12/99

RACE CAR LEGENDS

The Allisons
Mario Andretti
Crashes & Collisions
Demolition Derby
Drag Racing
Dale Earnhardt
Famous Finishes
Formula One Racing
A. J. Foyt
Jeff Gordon
History of NASCAR
Kenny Irwin Jr.
The Jarretts
The Labonte Brothers
The Making of a Race Car
Mark Martin
Jeremy Mayfield
Monster Trucks & Tractors
Motorcycles
Richard Petty
The Pit Crew
Stunt Driving
The Unsers
Rusty Wallace
Women in Racing

CHELSEA HOUSE PUBLISHERS

Ford
MAC TOOLS
Coca-Cola
Raybestos
The best in brakes
plasti-kote

KENNY IRWIN JR.

Ann Graham Gaines

CHELSEA HOUSE PUBLISHERS
Philadelphia

Frontis: *Kenny Irwin Jr., who won the NASCAR Raybestos Rookie of the Year award in 1998. The racing world agrees about his talent as a driver, and that the coming years will provide the experience he needs to become a true NASCAR Winston Cup contender.*

Produced by
21st Century Publishing and Communications, Inc.
New York, New York
http://www.21cpc.com

CHELSEA HOUSE PUBLISHERS

Editor in Chief: Stephen Reginald
Managing Editor: James D. Gallagher
Production Manager: Pamela Loos
Art Director: Sara Davis
Director of Photography: Judy L. Hasday
Senior Production Editor: LeeAnne Gelletly
Publishing Coordinator: James McAvoy
Assistant Editor: Anne Hill
Cover Illustration & Design: Keith Trego

Front Cover Photo: AP/Wide World Photos
Back Cover Photo: AP/Wide World Photos

The Chelsea House World Wide Website address is
http://www.chelseahouse.com

First Printing

1 3 5 7 9 8 6 4 2

Library of Congress Cataloging-in-Publication Data

Gaines, Ann.
  Kenny Irwin, Jr. / by Ann Gaines.
  64 p.   cm.—(Race car legends)
  Includes bibliographical references.
  Summary: A biography of the NASCAR driver who won the most points of any rookie on the Winston Cup circuit in 1998.
  ISBN 0-7910-5413-6
  1. Irwin, Kenny, 1969–   —Juvenile literature. 2. Automobile racing drivers
—United States—Biography—Juvenile literature. [1. Irwin, Kenny, 1969–   .
2. Automobile racing drivers.] I. Title. II. Series.
GV1032.I79G35 1999
796.72'092—dc21
[B]   99-31606
                                                                    CIP
                                                                    AC

CONTENTS

RACING IN INDIANAPOLIS

Indianapolis, Indiana, is the home of the famous race course known as the Brickyard. Every year on Memorial Day, hundreds of thousands of fans gather there to watch the Indianapolis 500-mile race. The race cars run on a 2.5-mile oval at close to 200 miles an hour, and the race is shown on television around the world. When the track was constructed in 1911, more than three million bricks—each weighing 10 pounds—were laid down as the surface of the track. Everyone started calling it the Brickyard. The Brickyard is now used only a couple of times each year, but another race track nearby is used almost every week.

For 20 years during the 1950s and 1960s, there had been dirt track racing every week in Indianapolis at a half-mile oval dirt track near the Brickyard. Those races had been stopped and the track had been built over. For a while, the only racing in Indianapolis took place on the one or two big weekends each year when a race came to the

A view of the Indianapolis Motor Speedway taken from the Goodyear blimp. More than three million bricks were used to make the surface of the track, hence earning it its nickname, the Brickyard.

The earliest auto races took place at county fairgrounds or dirt horse-racing tracks. Today thousands of fans fill the stands of huge facilities to watch their favorite drivers fly around the tracks at speeds close to 200 miles an hour.

Brickyard. So racing fans were glad when a new race track opened in Indianapolis just a mile or two from the Brickyard.

On April 27, 1997, about 15,000 people attended the opening of the Sixteenth Street Speedway. Like the Brickyard, it is also in the shape of an oval but is much smaller than the bigger track. The stands and even the cars that race there are smaller, and it has what is called a short track. Many old racing fans and now-famous drivers attended the opening that day. They were all happy to see the return of a sport they loved.

The fans quickly filled in the back rows of the stands and left the front rows for the younger and inexperienced dirt track fans. The wisdom of the old-timers quickly became evident when the racers started to practice laps around the course. The powerful cars would spray "rooster tails" of fine wet dirt behind them that would paint everything with a fine mud mist just like out of a paint sprayer. The fans sitting in the front few rows of the stands would get covered with mud as the cars sped by. They quickly moved to the back of the stands, now understanding the smiles on the veterans' faces.

Kenny Irwin Jr., a native of Indianapolis, was one of the professional racers who came for the celebration of the track's opening. The festivities were marked by a series of exciting races among veteran racers who had gone on to NASCAR (National Association for Stock Car Automobile Racing) racing, but who had returned to Indianapolis to drive the machines they grew up with. Kenny was officially a rookie on the NASCAR circuit that year. But he was certainly not a newcomer to racing. He had over 20 years' racing experience, from quarter midget races in cars not much more powerful than a lawnmower up to million-dollar racing machines capable of speeds close to 200 miles per hour.

That night in Indianapolis Kenny was joined by some of the other young racing stars who had grown up running races in the Midwest. Many of these outstanding and highly respected drivers looked at these races in Indianapolis as a sort of homecoming. Most of them had known and competed against each other for more than ten years. They knew each other's tricks.

The rules for the races that night at the Sixteenth Street Speedway were the same as those at a thousand dirt track races around the country every week. A one-lap qualifying race is run to select the fastest cars in case there are more cars that want to race than there are positions available. Then groups of eight to twelve cars run a series of four-lap races called "heats." The top four cars in each heat then move on to the final race, called the "feature" race. All of those who don't make it to the finals get to run a consolation race. The top four in that race also become finalists and join the others in the feature race.

Spraying dirt on the last few fans in the front rows who didn't know any better, or the kids who didn't care, the racers qualified and it was quickly decided who raced in which heat. Then the real show started. Drivers had hardly any place on the small course to pass other cars. There was only one fastest way around a curve; any other route would make the car go out of control. At this place, in each curve, the racers quickly cut a groove in the dirt with their tires. A car racing "in the groove" could go the fastest because the groove actually held the car in line as it turned the curve, sort of like a railroad track does for a train. The individual heats quickly became sprints for the corner grooves.

Although with such a short track the cars never had a chance to reach dangerous speeds, the racing was by no means short of excitement. There were always a lot of wrecks in each race. Drivers hit one another over and over again, bumping as they tried to be the first to reach the groove and jockeying for position. The racers always shouted to each other in a friendly way as they lined up for restarts. And there were many restarts, which occur when a wreck or spin-out blocks the course and everybody has to come to a halt. Restarts mean that everyone heads back to square one. Any advantage a car had gained is lost.

Kenny Irwin made it through the qualifying race. He started his first heat race in fine fashion, making a big move by the first corner, and jumping from seventh to fifth place. However, on the next lap, he scraped the wall coming around the back and gave back the two positions. Then Kenny craftily worked his way to fourth place and a position in the feature race by making quick sprints on each of the four successive restarts that followed. For the fans it was exciting racing to watch. Four more heats—all wild races, like Irwin's—determined the field for the final feature race. For this race Kenny started in the second row alongside Johnny Parsons III. They were behind Brian Gerster and Dave Darland on the front row.

At the start Gerster jumped into the lead, but Irwin followed him closely into turn one. Darland got inside of Irwin after the turn to claim the second spot. Daniel Doty quickly moved into fourth, and Jason Leffler, moving quite fast, had advanced into the fifth spot by the end of the first five laps. Things ran smoothly until the 10th lap. Then Doty appeared to make contact with another car, launching him into a spectacular flip that sent his car into the catch fence at the entrance to turn two. Because the first row of seats is only about

Johnny Parsons III, like Kenny Irwin, is a NASCAR driver who was also a popular and successful U.S. Auto Club midget and sprint car racer. Parsons started and raced side by side with Irwin at the grand opening of the new Sixteenth Street Speedway.

three feet behind the catch fence, some fans must have had a really frightful moment.

This crash brought out the race official's huge red flag, which signaled to all the drivers on the course they had to stop. Irwin had come to a halt facing the wrong way in turn three. Once they got the race restarted, there was little change. A few more wrecks were followed by a few more restarts. Despite all this, the top positions remained unchanged. As the end of the race neared, some drivers decided it was time to make their moves. Accelerating, Leffler and Irwin hit each other. While neither spun out, momentum forced both their cars into the infield. Nevertheless they each kept their motors running and zipped across the infield to rejoin the field. On the final restart, with four laps to go, Irwin was in eighth place. He finished fourth. In keeping with the theme of this feature race, three or four of the cars spun out after they crossed the finish line. It was a fun-filled night of racing for the fans and the drivers alike. Irwin had enjoyed a trip back to his hometown and the kind of race in which he had gotten his professional start.

THE LONG ROAD TO THE TOP

Kenneth D. Irwin Jr. was born in Indianapolis, Indiana, on August 5, 1969, to Reva and Kenneth D. Irwin Sr. He was the third of their four children, and their only boy. Early in life he started to go by the nickname Kenny. When he became a Winston Cup stock car racer, publicists and sportswriters started to refer to him simply as Kenny Irwin, but in his private life he still uses the Jr. in his name.

The Irwin family has always loved auto racing. When Kenny was growing up, his family owned a tool rental business, where both his mom and dad worked. After they sold the business in the mid-1990s, however, Kenneth Irwin Sr. fulfilled a life-long dream and started to build race cars for a living. Kenny's dad and both of his grandfathers have been huge race fans all their lives. While Kenny was growing up, his entire family not only went every year to see the Indianapolis 500 but also took many trips to see other races. "We never went on a vacation that wasn't to a racetrack," his mother

While Kenny Irwin was growing up in Indianapolis, his family always went to the Indianapolis 500 (as shown here in 1996). From his earliest childhood, Kenny and his father shared the dream that someday he would grow up and drive in that race.

15

remembers. From the time he was small both he and his dad dreamed that one day Kenny would grow up to race at Indy.

Kenny "loved anything with wheels from the time he could crawl," recalled Reva Irwin. As soon as he could reach the pedals on a Big Wheel, he always wanted to be outside, riding. She remembers having to watch him all the time because he wanted to go (in her opinion, not his) too far and too fast. When Kenny was five, his dad and mom bought him a quarter midget racer. Quarter midget race cars are exactly what their name indicates: they are race cars built to look like the popular midget racers teenagers and adults race on dirt or asphalt oval tracks all across the country. Only quarter midgets are exactly one-quarter the size of midgets and are powered by small horsepower Briggs engines or modified Honda motorcycle engines.

The sport started in southern California in the 1930s. Today there are over 3,000 teams of quarter midget racers throughout the United States and Canada. Kids can drive quarter midgets from the time they turn five until they are 16 years old. Three national championship events are held each year in late July, early August, and on Labor Day weekend.

Throughout his childhood, Kenny continued to race quarter midgets and then go-karts. As he grew, his dad started to build cars for him. The senior Kenneth also acted as his son's manager and coach. The family went to watch Kenny Jr. race practically every weekend. Always strong and a good athlete, he also became a star soccer player while in school. His mother remembers that she always pushed

him to develop other interests because she thought that he and his father would get too focused on racing. For example, she also made sure Kenny made time to go watch football games or attend homecomings.

When he was only 16, Kenny stopped racing go-karts and began racing stock cars. He started his stock car racing career by competing in races sponsored by the International Motor Sports Association (IMSA). IMSA was

As a boy, Kenny began to race quarter midget cars and then go-karts like the one pictured here. His father began to build his cars and took on the role of his son's manager and coach.

then in its heyday. Automobile manufacturers like Porsche, Jaguar, Nissan, and Toyota sponsored teams at IMSA's highest levels. At first Kenny raced stock cars he and his dad worked on.

By the time Kenny graduated from Lawrence North High School in Indianapolis in 1988, he had already been racing for thirteen years. He loved to tinker with cars and did so whenever he got a chance. After high school Kenny went to work in the family tool rental shop. He always had good business skills, including an ability to work with money, and he got along well with customers. During these years he also raced cars on a part-time basis. In 1988 he bought his first factory-built race car, a Brick Somerset GTO he raced in IMSA races.

In 1991 Kenny became a professional, full-time midget racer. By this time he was a full-grown man of 22. He'd reached his full size, standing 5' 11" and weighing about 160 pounds. Driving the car that his family owned and he and his dad had worked on, he took part in the United States Auto Club (USAC) midget series. Often he raced against Jeff Gordon, whose stepfather was good friends with Kenneth D. Irwin Sr.

Midgets are specially designed race cars that use full-sized automobile engines. They are what is called an open-wheel car, meaning their wheels aren't enclosed in fenders. They have no roofs and they burst with power. Racers take them around short dirt or asphalt courses for just a few miles. Midget racers start in a novice class and then, as they get more experience, they move through a series of stock classes. Every time Kenny took a small

Two open-wheeled cars hug the curve as they race around the track. During his five years as a midget racer Kenny earned a respectable record of 8 wins, 20 second-place finishes, 59 top-5 finishes, and 87 top-10 finishes.

step up in class, he found more new opponents and many new challenges. He had to race against better racers with more powerful equipment every time. He got to go faster and faster, which, of course, he loved.

Kenny stayed in professional midget racing for the next five years, through 1996, by which time he was 27. During his years as a midget racer he accumulated a record of 8 wins, 20 second-place finishes, 59 finishes in the top 5, and 87 finishes in the top 10. In 1994 he achieved one of his most memorable wins as a midget racer. In his hometown of Indianapolis he beat Mel Kenyon—a long-time midget racer with many victories to his credit—in the "Race of Champions" at the Mel Kenyon Classic.

In the midget series, as in other forms of auto racing, racers accumulate points for every race they run. The better they do in a race, the more points they earn. At the end of the season, the racer who has earned the most points in a series is named champion. In 1996 Irwin won more points than any other midget racer and became the USAC Skoal National Midget Series Champion.

Midget racing has also been the starting point of the careers of other present-day NASCAR stars. Jeff Gordon and Tony Stewart were Midget Series champions, Gordon in 1990 and Stewart in 1994 and 1995. By the time Irwin earned his championship, he had gotten used to at least a little fame. His victories had been covered by sportswriters in racing magazines. Midget racing fans crowded around to get his autograph.

When he got comfortable driving midget cars, Irwin set himself new goals. He wanted to try to work his way up through the ranks in racing and eventually reach the top. All his life Kenny has worked very hard at racing. After 1993 he not only drove midget cars but also raced sprint cars in the Stoops Freightliner/ USAC Sprint Car Series.

Sprint car drivers have a much more grueling schedule than midget racers. There are 70 events every year for sprint cars at 47 tracks in 23 states around the country, so sprint drivers spend a lot of time on the road. In return for their greater time commitment, they get an opportunity to earn more money than midget drivers. Over $9 million is awarded in prize money to sprint drivers every year.

Sprint cars race on short, oval dirt or asphalt tracks, measuring from 3/8- to 5/8-mile in length. Sprint cars are relatively light, weighing only about 1,200 pounds. They feature a tubular frame that completely encloses and protects the driver, who sits on top of the rear axle with his legs straddling a spinning drive shaft. The cars are powered by 410-cubic inch, 800-horsepower V8 engines. Both the blocks and the heads of these highly specialized engines are aluminum, and the valves are made of titanium. The engines do not burn gasoline, but use methanol instead. The two rear tires are huge and floppy, and they differ from each other in size since the cars only turn to the left as they speed around the oval tracks. Sprint cars can go from 60 to 120 miles an hour in four seconds and have a top speed of nearly 160 miles an hour.

Sprint car racing represents a real step up from midget car racing for an aspiring professional racer. Kenny quickly mastered sprint cars. He was the Stoops Freightliner/USAC Sprint Car Series Rookie of the Year in 1993, which meant he had the best record for the season of any rookie. After 1995 he raced a sprint car owned by Gus Hoffman. Altogether Irwin won seven races in the sprint series. Just as some NASCAR racers come up from midget racing, others learn their craft in sprint cars. A. J. Foyt, Mario Andretti, Bobby Unser, Al Unser, Parnelli Jones, Billy Vukovich, Tom Sneva, Johnny Rutherford, Gordon Johncock, Gary Bettenhausen, Pancho Carter, Johnny Parsons —the list of NASCAR drivers who once raced sprint cars seems to go on and on.

In 1994 Kenny Irwin started to race sprint

cars in another, more advanced series, called the Silver Crown Champion Series, which is also sponsored by the USAC. The Silver Crown series is run over a number of courses around the country and attracts the best sprint drivers. Its races have bigger purses than those in the Freightliner series. In 1994 Irwin made headlines when he won a big Silver Crown race called the Copper World Classic. Over the season he earned enough points to become the USAC Silver Crown Champion Series Rookie of the Year.

Kenny's best race in 1995 was the Tony Bettenhausen Memorial, where for a time he was in last position and then went on to win the race, earning $9,000. He also enjoyed an especially good year in 1996 when he won the USAC Triple Crown and finished second among all racers in points, just missing being named champion. His favorite race that year was at the Indianapolis Raceway in his hometown. There he led all 100 laps in the DuPont 100 and beat his long-time idol, Jimmy Sills.

In 1996 Irwin made another big step up. He started to drive in NASCAR truck races in addition to USAC events. On September 7, he drove a truck for Jim Herrick in a race at the Richmond International Raceway. He did so well that day—winning the pole in qualifying and coming in fifth overall—that in October Herrick signed Irwin to drive full-time for the NASCAR Craftsman Truck Racing series in 1997. Irwin would drive a truck sponsored by Ford, which was co-owned by Herrick and former basketball all-star Brad Daugherty. When he announced the signing, Herrick said, "This is a great day for Liberty Racing and

Ford." Reflecting on the fact that at age 27 Irwin had already racked up a total of 19 career victories, Herrick continued, asserting: "Kenny Irwin Jr. is one of the top young drivers in the business today."

Established in 1995, NASCAR truck racing is relatively new. However, it has proved a popular attraction. People like to see the powerful race cars that look like pick-up trucks racing at 140 miles an hour. The cars are really the same as those used in NASCAR Winston Cup or Busch Series racing, except that the engines are a little less powerful.

Kenny's first NASCAR race in the new season was on January 19, 1997, in Orlando, Florida. He came in seventh in the Chevy Truck Challenge. In the second race of the season, he did even worse, finishing 32nd. The third race was the Florida Dodge Dealers 400, which was held in Homestead, Florida. There Irwin started in fifth place. Throughout the race Irwin stayed close to the front, running almost always in the top five. However, five other drivers traded the lead in the first 114 laps. Finally, in lap 115, Kenny Irwin pulled out in front. A lap later, he fell back behind Jack Sprague. Sprague led the race for more laps than any other driver, but a flat tire eventually ruined his chances for a win. In lap 144, the race took a terrible turn when Joe Nemechek crashed his truck into a wall, and tragically sustained a brain injury in the wreck. The race officials put out the yellow caution flag, forcing all drivers to slow down while Nemechek's truck was moved from the course. Once they were allowed to get back up to speed, Irwin once again took the lead.

Racing fans love to watch NASCAR truck racing, which was first introduced in 1995. These race cars look like pick-up trucks and can go 140 miles an hour. The NASCAR truck series has always attracted both racing veterans and talented new drivers—many of whom go on to the Winston Cup. Kenny Irwin was named Rookie of the Year in the NASCAR truck series in 1997, beating out 12 other young drivers.

He led the pack from laps 154 to 162, slipped back for three laps, but then surged ahead for laps 166 and 167—the final two. Irwin won the race over Mike Bliss by a margin of less than a third of a second. His win netted him $44,750 and made him the first rookie to win a NASCAR truck race as well as the series' youngest winner ever.

Irwin drove in a total of 26 truck races that season. He had some bad days: he finished 28th in Watkins Glen, New York, and 31st in Sonoma, California. However, he also enjoyed another victory at the Pronto Auto Parts 400 in Fort Worth, Texas, in June. His margin of victory was slim at the Fort Worth race, as it was in Homestead: he finished under three-tenths of a second in front of Boris Said III. The Fort Worth race differed quite a bit from the Homestead race, however, in terms of speed. In Homestead Irwin had averaged only 98 miles per hour because of the many cautions in that race. At Fort Worth the average speed was 131 miles per hour. Irwin was beginning to reach the speeds he always seemed to thrive on.

Irwin finished his 1997 truck season 10th in final standings. This was great for a rookie. In fact, he earned enough points during the season to be named the NASCAR Craftsman Truck Series Rookie of the Year for 1997, beating out 12 other drivers. Kenny was quickly showing the big boys in racing that he was one to watch. Throughout his 20 years of racing he had kept getting better and more expensive cars to race. His truck races demonstrated he was ready to move on to another, even higher level.

ROBERT YATES
SIGNS KENNY IRWIN JR.

The very year Kenny Irwin won rookie of the year status in the NASCAR truck division, he also made it into stock car racing's big leagues when he joined the Winston Cup circuit in mid-season. In August 1997 a ceremony was held at the Brickyard in Irwin's home town of Indianapolis celebrating his joining Robert Yates's famous NASCAR racing team. The next year, Yates announced, Irwin would take over the seat in Yates's No. 28 Havoline Ford, which had been driven by Ernie Irvan. To get ready for 1999, Yates was going to enter a Ford Taurus, No. 27, in a few races with Irwin behind the wheel.

For years Irwin had dreamed of making such a step. His family had always stood behind him, helping him achieve his dreams. In fact, Kenny's family has always been immensely supportive of him in whatever he does. Throughout his career both his parents and his sisters would frequently travel to be with him when he raced. For the ceremony at the

---

Kenny Irwin talks with Robert Yates, who understands Winston Cup car engines better than almost anyone else in racing. Yates's teams run near the front of the Winston Cup pack year after year.

Brickyard, Kenny's friends, family, and fans turned out in force. His mother remembers the relief she felt that day, knowing he would get his big break racing stock cars rather than Indy cars. She considers stock car racing a much less dangerous sport than open-wheel Indy racing. Watching wrecks at Indy she had thought, "This is not good. This is not the right way [for my boy]." She would never forget the week earlier in his career when, racing in a midget race and two sprint races, he had to go to the hospital three times. Stock cars seem to her to be safer for Kenny to drive.

After the Yates announcement was made, sportswriter Curt Cavin, writing for the *Indianapolis Star/News*, called Irwin "young, adaptable, versatile and marketable." He quoted Robert Yates as saying, "He's our future."

Kenny Irwin had worked hard to get this position. Ernie Irvan had been driving car No. 28 for Yates. When rumors began to fly that Yates probably would not sign Irvan to a new contract in 1998, Kenny started to make a string of telephone calls to Yates's shop. Libby Gant, Yates's administrative assistant, quickly learned to recognize Kenny's voice. Irwin persisted. Yates apparently was impressed with the phone calls. He said, "If this guy hammers on the guy in front of him like he hammered on my telephone, they'll probably move over."

In joining Yates's team, Irwin had suddenly made it to the top of NASCAR racing. He not only would be driving in the Winston Cup series, on the toughest of all NASCAR circuits, but also would become a member of a very impressive team. Robert Yates's other driver is Dale Jarrett, a veteran racer with a lot of wins

to his name. Jarrett won the Daytona 500 in 1993 and 1996. In 1997 he was second among all Winston Cup drivers in terms of points earned racing. He is expected to keep racing for years.

Irwin's car, No. 28, was equally impressive. Some stock car fans cheer for a particular driver. Others root for a particular make of car, or the car bearing a particular number. (In reality, stock car owners own several cars labeled with the same number. The cars look identical, decorated exactly alike, but they each

When Kenny started driving Robert Yates's No. 28 Havoline Ford, he became a member of a very impressive team. During this pit stop at the Michigan Speedway in 1998, Irwin's pit crew changes four tires and fills the car with gas in about 20 seconds.

run a little differently. The Winston Cup circuit includes races on short tracks, roads, and superspeedways. One car will be adjusted so that it runs better on the short tracks, for example. Another will be adjusted for superspeedways—perhaps even just one particular superspeedway. Others stand by, ready, in case a car is wrecked.

Irwin's No. 28 had been driven for years by the late Davey Allison, who was the victor at Daytona in 1992. Then it was driven by Ernie Irvan, another frequent winner. Talking about the car, Kenny Irwin said, "I probably feel more pressure knowing what the 28 car has done in the past. I've been watching it for years. It's got a lot of history."

And his new boss was something of a legend as well. Robert Yates was born in North Carolina on April 19, 1943. Yates is known as the best engine builder on the circuit. His cars are noted for their phenomenal acceleration out of the corners of a race course. Just as Kenny had to pay his dues to become a driver, so Robert Yates paid his dues as a builder of race car engines. He started at the bottom of a team of legendary stock car engine wizards more than thirty years ago.

In 1968 Yates got a job working on the motors of the Holmon Moody cars. In 1971 he went to work for Junior Johnson, a dominating driver and champion during the '60s and '70s who had also driven for Holmon Moody. In 1972 Yates prepared the motors for Bobby Allison, who was working for and learning from Junior Johnson. The season when Yates worked on the motors was the season that Allison won 10 races and had 24 top-three finishes.

Yates moved to the DiGard racing team in 1976, where he worked for 10 years building the motors for such stars as Darrell Waltrip and Ricky Rudd. His cars won over 40 races during that time. Few people realize that it was Yates who provided the engine that Richard Petty used in his 200th career win at Daytona in 1984.

Yates bought the team from Harry Ranier in 1987, and it became known as the Robert Yates Racing Thunderbirds. Since 1996 he has been entering two race cars in every Winston Cup race, No. 88 and No. 28. Today Robert Yates cars are known as some of the fastest cars on the circuit, and each year Yates and his team's sponsors spend millions of dollars on them. When Irwin signed on with Yates, he would get some of the biggest sponsors in the game— Texas, Havoline, MAC Tools, Raybestos, and Coca Cola.

Kenny Irwin had to make some big adjustments when he joined Yates's team. Much more would be expected of him. Winston Cup drivers may only race 33 times annually, but they work far more than 33 days a year. They spend a lot of time in their owners' shops, consulting with their crew chiefs and others about their cars' handling. Every time they race, they spend two or three days at a course, testing a car and qualifying it. They make a lot of public appearances, meeting fans at races, going to press conferences, and talking to sportswriters. Throughout the year they attend functions for their sponsors, meeting corporate executives, for example. So in joining Yates's team, Irwin would become something of a celebrity. He was assigned a publicist to handle

NASCAR drivers make a lot of promotional appearances, which was a new experience for Kenny Irwin. Here he joins a 1999 Coca-Cola promotion that would give racing fans a chance to ride in a stock car around Atlanta Motor Speedway with the sport's top drivers. Pictured (from left) are Tony Stewart, Ricky Rudd, Jason Jarrett, Ned Jarrett, Irwin, Bill Elliott, Dale Jarrett, Kyle Petty, Adam Petty, and Jeff Burton.

public relations for him. He had to get used to living in the public eye.

He also had to get used to working with a large group of new people. Robert Yates was the owner of Irwin's car and his team manager. But Yates employed more than 80 people to work on Irwin's car. The Ford Tauruses Irwin would take over were very powerful machines. They were all powered by Ford single-cam, pushrod actuated, overhead valve V8 engines, measuring 358 cubic inches. The NASCAR Winston Cup race cars that race at Daytona or Talladega may look like the Ford or Chevrolet family car parked in the driveways of your neighborhood, but the only things they have in common are the hood, roof top, and the deck lid. All of the other parts of the car are handmade specially. To sum up, every time he started the ignition on the No. 28 Havoline ford, Irwin would be assuming responsibility for a car valued in the hundreds of thousands of dollars, and which had taken more than a dozen people many weeks to make.

WINSTON CUP
ROOKIE OF THE YEAR

Kenny Irwin's first Winston Cup race was the Exide NASCAR Select Batteries 400 held at the Richmond International Raceway in September 1997. He drove a Robert Yates Ford Taurus labeled No. 27. To decide the race's starting positions, Winston Cup events start with qualifying rounds in which drivers start from a standstill at the pit stop. When they pass the finish line their first time around, they reach full speed and take two laps just as fast as they can go. The fastest among all the qualifiers gets to start on the pole, or in the first spot. Irwin practically flew during his qualifying round at Richmond. He ran second fastest among all the drivers, which meant he got to start the race in the second position, on what is called the outside pole. It was a great start to a new phase in his career.

The Richmond race proved very exciting for Irwin, too. On lap 21 he was running close to the front of the pack when suddenly his car touched that of Jeff Burton. Burton spun out. Three drivers

---

Kenny Irwin was named Rookie of the Year in his first Winston Cup season. In the last race of 1998 at Atlanta Motor Speedway (pictured here), he started the race on the pole for the first time. He was the only rookie to lead a race that season.

35

right behind him—Ernie Irvan, Mark Martin, and Hut Stricklin—got tangled up trying to avoid hitting Burton. Irwin sped on. Burton finally got turned around, but by this time he had fallen back to 40th place. In lap 86, Irwin took the lead from Bobby Hamilton and kept it for 12 laps. By lap 116, Burton, the very driver Irwin had bumped, was in the lead. He led until lap 283 and then regained the lead again when Joe Nemechek gave it up to make a pit stop. Toward the very end of the race, at lap 361, Irwin's teammate Dale Jarrett passed Burton. Jarrett held on and won the race. Having started 23rd, Jarrett came from the farthest back among all winners to date in the season. Irwin got what sportswriter David Poole called a "solid eighth." He earned $17,825 for two hours and 45 minutes' work.

This race made Irwin the only rookie in modern NASCAR history to start on the front row and lead the pack in his first Winston Cup race. That race seems likely to remain one of Irwin's favorite memories.

His second start was the Haynes 500 at Martinsville, Virginia. He started in third place and stayed in the top 10 for most of the race, but a broken fuel pump finally cut him out of the real competition. He finished 37th. He would go on to appear in two more Winston Cup races in 1997. At the same time he was still racing NASCAR trucks as well. In October both he and Ernie Irvan—whose place Irwin was taking on Yates's team—entered a truck race at California Speedway. By the final lap the two were battling for third place. Several times they bumped into each other. Finally Irwin inched ahead of Irvan and came

in third. Even in the cool-down lap, Irwin and Irvan continued to ram each other. In the garage after the race, they angrily shouted at each other. Irvan pushed Irwin. Afterwards Irvan said, "I'm just not really happy about Kenny Irwin."

By the end of the 1997 Winston Cup season, Kenny had already proved to be one of the fastest drivers in qualifying for starting positions each week. Everyone on the Robert Yates

Kenny climbs out of his car after clinching the pole position at the 1998 NAPA 500. To win the pole he had qualified fastest, with an average speed of 193.461 miles an hour. Although Kenny had no wins during the 1998 season, his one top-five finish and four top-10 finishes helped make him Rookie of the Year.

Kenny (right) talks with crew chief Richard Labbe. Good communication between the driver and the crew is essential in a winning team.

Team was really impressed with the young man and looking forward to 1998.

The Winston Cup season starts in February of each year. The first race is always held at Daytona, Florida, the birthplace of stock car racing and NASCAR itself. The Daytona 500 is the most famous of all the stock car races. It's challenging, too. The cars go extremely fast, at speeds of over 190 miles an hour, around a big 2.5-mile oval that is banked (it rises) over 30 degrees on the turns.

Racing in the first 125-mile qualifying race, Kenny was involved in the first crash of the 1998 Winston Cup season. On lap 33 of the scheduled 50, Kenny brushed the outside wall coming out of turn two. His car shot back toward the infield and struck Todd Bodine's No. 35 car, which was running alongside. Bodine's car then hit Dick Trickle's No. 90. All three drivers ended up unhurt but unhappy. It occurred so fast that Kenny didn't even know what happened. Interviewed right after his attempt to qualify, he said, "I was having a ball out there until that mishap in turn two. I honestly don't know what happened out there. I can't wait to watch the tape myself. I was just trying to stay in line. I was on the outside and the 35 car was trying to get in, but I don't know if he affected the air and that's what got me in the fence or what."

Bodine and Trickle were mad at first that they had been forced out of the race by a rookie, but they soon calmed down. Sometimes drivers are not so understanding when they are hurt by rookie mistakes.

Irwin's poor showing in the qualifying round meant he started the Daytona 500 in 39th position. He raced well enough to move a long way up, and his was the 19th car to cross the finish line, a whole lap behind the leader, Dale Earnhardt.

Daytona would not be the only course where Kenny Irwin experienced frustration in the spring of 1998. He finished 36th at Las Vegas,

39th at Darlington, 43rd at Bristol, 39th in Texas, and 40th at Talladega. The list of poor showings seemed to go on and on. His car failed to qualify for the Coca-Cola 600 at Charlotte on May 24, marking the first time the No. 28 car failed to qualify for a race since Yates took over ownership of the team. Kenny simply could not go fast enough. At the end of the season he would look back on Charlotte as his biggest disappointment.

The week after Charlotte, at the race in Dover, Delaware, Kenny qualified in the ninth spot on the one-mile banked oval track traveling at around 150 miles an hour. But once the race started, the car didn't handle very well. Irwin's pit crew made small adjustments in tire pressure, suspension, and handling. But nothing would make the car fast or stable. He finished a very disappointing 33rd place. After Dover, Kenny explained what he was learning, that natural talent at driving alone wasn't enough to guarantee a good showing in a Winston Cup race. "We qualified pretty good for our first race here but struggled during the race. We just couldn't get the set up right. It's difficult here because you really don't know what you need until you make a 100-lap run. You have to kind of figure out how to really race the race track."

Here he used "you" to mean the whole team. How to race a track is the joint responsibility of a group of people, including the driver, the pit chief and crew, and the car's mechanics. Irwin was also discovering that he couldn't always communicate very well with the crew and mechanics about how the car was actually handling and what he thought was wrong with it. So they weren't always able to make the corrections and adjustments that were required. Kenny said, "The driver sitting in the seat helps make the cars better, and the more experience I get the more I will be able to help. I look to Dale Jarrett when we go to test and he can do that. I say why can't I, you know. It's just time figuring that stuff out."

Yates echoed Irwin's sentiments. He said, "It certainly helps when the driver understands the physics of these things. We're not allowed to put computers in here when we're testing and practicing. It's so important that the driver can give you good feedback."

Irwin had one more terrible day in his 1998 season. Race 27 on the Winston Cup circuit is held on a tight, small oval track only a little more than a half-mile in length at Martinsville, Virginia. Ernie Irvan was the fastest qualifier there, clocking in at 193.6 miles an hour for the race on September 27, 1998. That day high temperatures proved nearly unbearable. Irwin dropped out of the race after 175 laps because of heat exhaustion. The eventual winner, Ricky Rudd, had similar problems. The cooling system in Rudd's driving suit broke after only five laps of the race and he endured a temperature of 150 degrees for the hundreds of laps that remained. Afterward Robert Yates talked about Irwin's season. He said, "We're anxious. We're impatient. We're probably a little bit greedy, but we want to win some races and get going here. . . . We want to be racing in the top 10 every week."

The 1998 season indeed held some incredibly

down moments for Irwin. But it was hardly all like that. Yates's hope that Irwin would eventually win races in fact seemed quite reasonable. In April Kenny Irwin finished fifth in a race at Atlanta. He would have done even better except that a lug nut had fallen onto the floor and had to be hunted down during a pit stop. He finished ninth in the race in Richmond in June.

In mid-season Robert Yates sent Kenny to the Bondurant Driving School in Phoenix, Arizona, to practice his skills for twisty, flat road courses like those at Sears Point and Watkins Glen. When he had been racing trucks, Kenny had had a lot of trouble with the road courses. He was not used to the many gear changes the twisty tracks demanded. He explained why they sent him to the school, saying, "The main reason I went out there was to get refreshed with the heel-and-toe technique so you can use the clutch more."

That schooling really paid off for Kenny. He finished ninth at the 350-mile Sears Point race on June 28. Sears Point has a total of 10 turns, both left and right. Irwin handled them professionally. On September 12 he got his fourth top-10 finish of the year, coming in 10th in the Exide 400, the 25th race in the by-then extremely exhausting season. He went on to finish 11th in two Winston Cup races later that season, coming just shy of being considered a leader. He ended the 1998 season on a very high note when he qualified fastest in the last race of the season and started on the pole for the first time in his very short Winston career.

In 1998 Jeff Gordon won a total of 13 of the Winston Cup races and was named the series

champion for the season. It was a tremendous achievement for both Gordon and his chief engineer Ray Evernham. By the end of the year Gordon had made 33 starts, earned a total of 5,328 points, and won $6,175,867 altogether. Mark Martin was Gordon's closest competitor. Martin earned 4,964 points in 33 starts, had 22 top-five finishes, and won

During the 1998 season, Kenny attended the Bondurant Driving School in Phoenix, Arizona, where, among other things, he refreshed his heel-and-toe technique.

While at the Bondurant Driving School, in the middle of the 1999 season, Kenny worked on the many gear changes required on twisting, flat road courses. The refresher course seemed to pay off when Kenny ended the season with four top-10 finishes.

$3,279,370. Between the two of them, Gordon and Martin won well over half of all Winston Cup races.

Kenny Irwin finished the 1998 season in 28th position among all NASCAR drivers with 2,760 points. He started in 32 races. He had no wins, one top-five finish, and four top-10 finishes. He won $1,433,567. His point total automatically made him Rookie of the Year. Sportswriters agreed that as far as rookie seasons go, his had actually been a real winner.

He was the only rookie to appear in 32 races and lead a race in 1998. He was the leading rookie at the end of the race 14 times. No other rookie had even a single top-10 finish. At the beginning of the season, sportswriters and fans had seen him as being in competition with rookies Kevin LePage, Steve Park, and Jerry Nadeau. But he had beaten all three handily. Irwin took great pride in his trophy.

AFTER
THE AWARD

Winning the Rookie of the Year award ended Kenny Irwin's first season on the Winston Cup circuit on a very positive note. But you only get to be a rookie once, and he never enjoyed a win in 1998. In 1999 he had to set new goals for himself. At the beginning of the new racing year, NASCAR Online, the official NASCAR Internet site, summed up the stock car racing world's opinion of him. "That's not to say Irwin didn't run well," NASCAR Online said about his lack of wins. Looking to the future, it went on, "You can bet he'll climb in '99. . . . Irwin is learning this game, and learning pretty quickly. The Raybestos Rookie of the Year is growing into the famous No. 28 Texaco car."

At the end of the 1998 season, Kenny explained his and the team's long-term goals. He reported, "Robert [Yates] and I didn't sit down at the start of the year and say this is what we want to achieve as

Winning Rookie of the Year in 1998 was a triumph for Kenny Irwin and the Robert Yates team. But Kenny's second NASCAR season required some new goals and changes so that he and the team could go on to even greater achievements.

building. What is amazing is that the cars are capable of going much faster than they actually do. NASCAR has ruled that at the superspeedways the speeds must be regulated. Otherwise it would be simply too dangerous for both the race teams and the spectators.

To limit the racer's speed at Daytona, a metal plate with four small holes in it, called a restrictor plate, is placed between the carburetor and the intake manifold. This limits how much air and fuel is exploded in the cylinders in each cycle of the engine's revolution. One effect of these restrictor plates is that all of the cars are limited to the same top speed, and they all can get to that speed at about the same rate. Everything that happens during the race is done at very close to full speed. During the race, cars break off into packs that are so close together that the air rushing over the first car creates a draft that pulls the others on. Any car that wants to pass another has to drop out of the chain and survive the sledge hammer blow of the open air, and not wreck. That's the tricky part.

At Daytona in 1999, Kenny started the race in the back at the 41st position. His car had performed well during the qualifying heats, but he had finished 16th in a race where only the top 15 finishers progressed. The team had an exemption that could be used to allow it to compete, but using an exemption means you begin at the end. Once the main event started, Kenny immediately made real progress. The few changes the race team had made to the car overnight were exactly right. On lap 15, Kenny was in 31st place; on lap 30, he was 21st. The

11 fastest cars ran in front in their own pack. This kind of racing takes daring and skill. In sprint racing, where most of the new NASCAR racers come from, the car has so much power that racing often becomes a sequence of sliding, turning, braking, and accelerating. In contrast, in Daytona racing, where everyone has the same incredible power, a winning driver needs

Kenny (right) celebrates with his crew after setting a new course record during a qualifying round at the Texas Motor Speedway in March of 1999. His record-breaking speed was 190.154 miles an hour.

Kenny Irwin, driving the Havoline Ford (center), narrowly escapes a multi-car pileup. In NASCAR races, cars that want to pass may find themselves driving three across at speeds around 190 miles an hour. Drivers have to use all their maneuvering skills to avoid deadly collisions.

to be cool, trusting, and patient, making split-second decisions and executing them calmly while under tremendous pressure.

In the early laps of the 1999 Daytona 500, Bobby Labonte and Jeff Gordon battled for the lead. Kenny ran in a second pack following a few seconds behind the leaders. On lap 40, Kenny was 15th overall. He had passed 26 other cars to be there. It was obvious that

Kenny's car was fast enough to win. Could the team make the right pit stops at the right moments? Could they take advantage of any tiny chance fate handed them to get ahead? Was the car going to last? Kenny was up to 12th overall on lap 47. On lap 49, Kenny was 11th with Dale Earnhardt right in front of him. Kenny quickly made a pit stop for four new tires and fuel, as did most of the cars between laps 53 to 60.

During Kenny's pit stop, they changed the tire pressure by one pound. Kenny went into pit row in 11th place and came out in 15th. Not too bad at all. After the first pit stops, Rusty Wallace and Dale Jarrett were running at the front. Kenny moved up to eighth by the halfway point in the race. Dale Jarrett, the other Yates Racing Team driver, was second. On lap 118, Kenny was fifth and Dale third. Kenny dropped to 11th in a heartbeat, as he slowed to avoid a wreck in front of him. By lap 130 Kenny had moved back to eighth.

In between turns three and four on lap 134, the cars were three across. Dale Jarrett was on the outside of Kenny, who was in the middle of the pack. Dale signaled Kenny to let him in from the outside line to the middle. Kenny saw Dale coming and quickly lifted his foot from the accelerator to slow down just the tiniest bit to let Dale squeeze in. It was an extremely daring move by Dale. He would have to leave the slipstream of the outside pack, take the hit of the air between the two rows of cars, and slip into Kenny's pack close enough not to break the draft. It was a disaster, Kenny later said. "I don't know if we actually

Kenny Irwin's NASCAR career continues to blossom, and he shows every sign of becoming a racing champion. Liked by fans, Kenny autographs the hat of one admirer.

touched or if the air just got off his spoiler and he spun. I have no idea, but I feel very, very bad about it, if it was my fault."

Whether or not Kenny touched it, Dale's car moved down to the level bottom of the track and then started to slide back up the banked track, into the path of the outside line of cars coming at over 190 miles an hour. Dale's car hit the outside wall and started to spin around and around. It flipped over onto its roof and slid back down the track, where it was hit by many other cars. It came to rest on its wheels in the grass infield of the track. Miraculously Dale crawled out of the mangled mess and walked away. It was a spectacular wreck that forced 12 cars out of the race. But not Kenny, who sped away from the pack untouched. The yellow caution flag came out, and the cars were forced to hold their positions in the race until the dead cars and the debris could be cleared away from the track.

On lap 178 there was another caution flag. Rusty Wallace, who had led the race for 104 laps, and Jeremy Mayfield stayed on the track while the rest of the leaders including Kenny Irwin, Jeff Gordon, and Dale Earnhardt came into the pits for four fresh tires. The new tires soon made a difference. Wallace and Mayfield had not opened up enough of a lead on the others to keep them far behind. Earnhardt, who was eighth at the restart, quickly jumped to third. Gordon passed him for second a couple of laps later and settled in behind Rusty. On lap 188 Gordon dropped low onto the track to pass Rusty Wallace, and right in front of him was Ricky Rudd, who was a lap behind the leaders. Gordon quickly wrenched the steering wheel to avoid a rear-end collision. The crowd gasped as Jeff passed Ricky and Rusty by inches, going 190 miles an hour to take over first place. The rest of the pack of leaders, led by Dale Earnhardt, also passed Wallace to set up the exciting conclusion to the race.

For the last 12 laps, Earnhardt tried every way he could think of to pass Gordon, but Jeff had just gotten four new tires and his car handled exceptionally well. Jeff Gordon finally beat Dale Earnhardt, even if only by 0.128 seconds. After the race, Gordon said, "Man! I want to thank Dale for a great race. He did everything he possibly could. He's probably going to tell you I learned too much from him. He's taught me a lot of things in the last couple of years and that's the only way I kept him behind me." Earnhardt told an interviewer, "I just couldn't get to him. He was . . . holding the air between us. I knew that, but I couldn't [do anything about it]. Every time I'd back off, he'd back off." In other words, every time Gordon looked in his rearview mirror and saw Earnhardt slowing so that he could escape the air stream and pass Gordon, Gordon would slow, too.

Kenny Irwin had the best seat in the house to watch and learn these little tricks from the seasoned professionals. He sat in third place, immediately behind Dale. "Earnhardt was doing everything he could to get by Gordon. If he had had the lane, I would have probably gone with him. . . . I felt like if he went I could probably end up second and progressively move up. That's what I did for the last 10 laps, just try to make the right moves just to keep inching up for the end of the race."

Kenny and the crew were happy to get third. Sportswriter Bill Frederickson expressed his surprise at how well Irwin had done there. "Kenny Irwin, who piloted his No. 28 Texaco/Havoline Ford to the third-place position, wasn't supposed to be there," Frederickson wrote in an article he submitted to NASCAR Online. "After all," he went on, "Irwin was running only his second Daytona 500. He was starting just his 37th career series event. And he used a provisional to make the field, at that."

Irwin gloried in his best run ever. He came away from Daytona with his belief in himself confirmed. "We felt like we had a very good race in our Gatorade 125 [the qualifying race], and we finished 16th. We came back, and we said what do we need to do? We made very minor changes, really, to the car. I think that [the third place finish] does a lot for our team. Our team has gone through a lot over the winter, and it's going to help make everybody and myself more confident going into the whole year. We've just got to get more consistent and get a lot more top-threes."

Kenny and the crew won $465,084 for the race and 165 points toward the year-end championship. Kenny had done much better than anyone had expected, with the possible exception of himself.

The next week Kenny finished in the top 10. However, he must have sometimes continued to feel as if his career were a roller coaster ride. The week after that Kenny totally destroyed a No. 28 car in a wreck. Then he was on his way up again. At Texas Motor Speedway on March 28, 1999, during a qualifying round, he set a new speed record for the course, racing at 190.154 miles per hour, four miles faster than the old record of 185.906 miles an hour.

Kenny Irwin seems poised for great things. In the event that things don't work out, in case he doesn't become the champion he believes he could be, he has saved a great deal of money. He could go into business, should an injury, for example, take him out of racing. He could build race cars, like his dad has. But what Kenny Irwin Jr. dreams of is racing for decades to come. Stock car racers often enjoy long careers, among the longest in the sports world. Kenny Irwin's name will no doubt remain in the headlines for many years to come.

CHRONOLOGY

1969   Kenneth D. Irwin Jr. born August 5 in Indianapolis, Indiana.

1974   Starts racing quarter midgets and then go-karts.

1985   Starts racing in International Motor Sports Association (IMSA).

1988   Graduates from high school; works at family retail tool shop; races part-time.

1991   Becomes professional, full-time, midget racer; enters U.S. Auto Club (USAC) National Midget Series.

1993   Is named Rookie of the Year in the USAC Sprint Car Series.

1994   Is named Rookie of the Year in the USAC Silver Crown Sprint Series.

1996   Finishes second in points in the USAC Silver Crown Championship Series; wins the USAC Skoal National Midget Series.

1997   Wins two races, finishes 10th overall for the season, and is named Rookie of the Year in the NASCAR Truck Series; signs contract with Robert Yates to drive Yates's Ford Taurus No. 28 on the NASCAR Winston Cup circuit in the next season.

1998   Wins the most points of any rookie on the Winston Cup circuit and receives Rookie of the Year trophy; finishes the season 28th overall, having earned over $1 million through the year.

1999   Finishes third in the very first Winston Cup race of the new season, the Daytona 500, amazing the auto racing world.

STATISTICS

NASCAR TRUCK SERIES

YEAR	RACES	WINS	TOP 5	TOP 10	WINNINGS
1997	26	2	7	10	$302,870

NASCAR WINSTON CUP SERIES

YEAR	RACES	WINS	TOP 5	TOP 10	WINNINGS
1997	4	0	0	1	61,230
1998	32	0	1	4	1,433,567
1999 (as of 6/24)	15	0	1	2	1,099,014
NASCAR CAREER (as of 6/24)	**77**	**2**	**9**	**17**	**$2,896,681**

FURTHER READING

Brinster, Richard. *Jeff Gordon.* Philadelphia: Chelsea House Publishers, 1997.

Center, Bill, ed. *NASCAR: The Thunder of America, 1948–1998.* New York: HarperCollins, 1998.

Golenbock, Peter. *American Zoom: Stock Car Racing from the Dirt Tracks to Daytona.* New York: Macmillan, 1994.

Golenbock, Peter. *The Last Lap: The Life and Times of NASCAR's Legendary Heroes.* New York: Macmillan, 1998.

Hunter, Don. *American Stock Car Racers.* Osceola, WI: Motorbooks International, 1997.

The Official NASCAR Handbook: Everything You Want to Know about the NASCAR Winston Cup Series. New York: HarperCollins, 1998.

Stephenson, Sallie. *Winston Cup Racing.* New York: Crestwood House, 1991.

Wukovits, John F. *The Composite Guide to Auto Racing.* Philadelphia: Chelsea House Publishers, 1998.

ABOUT THE AUTHOR

Ann Graham Gaines is a freelance author and photo researcher who lives in the woods near Gonzales, Texas, with her four children.

INDEX